Amish Canning & Preserving Cookbook for Beginners:

Simple and Delicious Homemade Recipes for Fruit and Pie Fillings, Pickles, and Sweet Spreads That Everyone Can Enjoy

By
Guinevere White

Table of Contents

Introduction

Food is a crucial part of our survival. What we choose to eat is a true reflection of our culture, values, norms, and traditions. Along with eating, preserving the food is also necessary. In today's modern society, many of us indulge in bad eating habits, which likely creates the urge to go back to the simple lifestyle with much more concentration on home-cooked meals that provide true joy, away from the hustle of modern society. The more and more we indulge in a simple lifestyle, the more we are getting tied to our old values, traditions, and healthy ways of our forebears.

Our grandmother shares enough knowledge and tools to care for our families, the way we lived, and the food choices we made. Learning about food canning is one of the irreplaceable techniques passed to us from our ancestors.

In the past, food canning used to be the most common household duty performed by housewives. The technique of canning is not at all new, as it has been around for thousands of years. Our great grandfathers used to harvest the food that was then stored by housekeepers to feed their families in winters when the garden and farms were bare.

Now, with the ease of grocery stores, and food becoming industrialized, anyone can find inexpensive canned food anytime they want. Thus, home canning becomes much of a sideway process. But with the popularity of healthy eating and home-cooked meals, canning has also become a new buzz in the town.

As the name of this book suggests, the focus is to improve knowledge about Amish canning, and to learn different home canning techniques. So, if you have never canned food, then this book will help you to gain some experience of this technique.

The Amish are an amazing and fascinating group of people who are famous for their simple lifestyle, ways of living, and eating. Their beliefs and simplicity are the reason they grow their food and then love to preserve their harvest.

The Amish are skillful when it comes to preserving food, and one main reason for canning food is that it allows them to preserve all the seasonal food, so it is readily available throughout the year.

This book also covers canning recipes, so you must keep reading. Whether you have been canning food for quite a long time, or trying it for the first time, our recipes will soon fill your kitchen pantry with colorful, delicious, and vibrant preserved food items. The recipes introduced in this cookbook will surely please you, and your whole family.

Now you can get the joy of eating canned food but also get the pleasure of seeing those preserved food jars sitting in your kitchen pantry. The home-canned food is a great choice over store-bought canned food, as the freshness and quality are in your own hands.

Versatile, vibrant, and joyful canned food is what this cookbook is all about. All the canned recipes are prepared straight from the heart, into the jar, and right onto your dining tables.

The purpose of this cookbook is to make canning an adoptive and easy affair.

This comprehensive book includes the following:

- The Basics of Amish Canning
- What Are the Amish People Religious Beliefs or Traditions?
- Types of Food that Amish Can
- History of Canning
- Benefits of Canning
- Tools and Supplies Needed
- How to Fit Canning in Your Life
- Methods of Food Preservation
- Types of Canning
- Food Acidity and the Ways to Process
- Ways to Save On Canning Lids
- How to Reuse Canning Lids
- Sterilization of Canning
- How to Spot a Canned Good That Has Expired
- Basic Tips for Success during Canning Food
- General Guidelines for Canning
- Do's and Don'ts of Canning
- Recipes (Fruits, Pie Fillings, Jams, Jellies, Spreads, Meat, Fish, Chicken, Soup, Pickles)

Learning something new is a very enjoyable process, as it allows one to push their limits and try something unique. This book is no doubt brimming with the philosophy of making the canning process as easy as possible. Canning is an enjoyable process, and an art, especially if you grow your fruits and vegetables, then it is an awesome idea to save the harvest. No doubt, home-canned food is much better than store-bought canned food. Working with your own hands brings joy and complete satisfaction when feeding the family. The Amish Canning book serves as an old homemaker technique that fits well in a modern kitchen. So, let's start with the basics.

1

The Basics of Amish Canning

This chapter of the book helps the readers to learn the basics about the Amish lifestyle, their origins, and traditions. As you move forward, you will get a glimpse of traditional Amish canning. First, let us look into the Amish lifestyle.

Amish Lifestyle

The Amish belong to the southern part of Switzerland and Germany. They settled in the United States in the 19th century, on the eastern side of Pennsylvania, Lowe, Ohio, Indiana, and Kansas.

The Amish lifestyle is very simple as they avoid electricity and rarely use high means of transportation and prefer bicycles for riding. They respect their cultural values and family traditions.

They prefer growing their fruits and vegetables and purchase only flour and sugar from grocery stores.

As Amish are into farming and harvesting, they are also very skillful in canning all the harvested fruits, vegetables, and even meat for wintertime when their gardens are no longer producing fruits or vegetables.

The process of canning is a staple in their community, as preserving food for the winter months is more of a necessity. The Amish families are preparing food for the winter months, and spring food, by using a method of canning for generations. Canning is a great technique to seal and pack the food into glass jars, making it a great preserved food to be consumed all year long.

With the new and modern appliances, techniques, and methods introduced, a lot of non-Amish people use dishwashers to prepare the jar for sealing the food. But the Amish community is still stuck with old traditions that you can learn in the next few parts of this book.

A Guide to the Amish Way of Life

The Amish are simple and plain people who are living in the USA, following a traditional Christian church, driving from Swiss Germany. Lancaster country, Pennsylvania, is the center of the Amish, and it is where they live.

The Amish people are known for three things: a simple lifestyle, simple clothing, and avoiding any modern technology. The Amish do not drive automobiles, and their means of transportation are usually bicycles. They are not connected to electricity, but they do rely on solar or wind power.

Regarding education, the higher level of education is discouraged, as according to the Amish community it leads to social segregation. Almost 30 percent of the Amish are in farming and others are into trade and businesses.

Because of religious and cultural reasons, the Amish do not like connecting to people of the outer worlds. The Amish lifestyle is based on their religious values and beliefs. They are strongly devoted to traditions and cultures. The use of horse-drawn buggies, the dressing, and manner are often considered outdated for any non-Amish modern person. While the Amish life is unimaginable for a lot of us, they still cherish and embrace it fully.

History of the Amish

The history of Amish people resides back to the 16th century in Europe when they were known to be Swiss brethren.

The Amish culture, or Amish, is a term that is named after Jakob Ammann, who was a Mennonite leader from the 17th to 18th century. When Amish people faced religious oppression in Europe, they immigrated to the United States in the 8th century. Some of the Amish stayed in Europe and joined the Mennonite groups. In the middle of the 19th century, the Amish communities got into a dispute about adopting modern technologies, and this split them into two groups. One group named itself Amish Mennonites, while the other goes with the traditional title of Old Order Amish.

What Are the Amish People Religious Beliefs or Traditions?

The Amish believe in one God. Their faith and belief are what lead them to adopt a simple lifestyle. They are disciplined people and hard-working as well. They care about calmness, practicality, and care for humanity. They follow the word of the bible, which is to them the word of God. Adult baptism is a tradition that is still followed. The most popular holidays that Amish celebrate are religious holidays as well as Easter, Thanksgiving, Ascension Day, Pentecost, Christmas, Good Friday, and Whit Monday.

Amish Thoughts About Modern Technology

They are not conformable with the outer world and modern technology, so they shun modern conveniences as it goes against their religious beliefs.

The Amish do not have cars for transportation; they do not use mobiles, TV, computers, or radios.

They may accept a ride from someone who does have a car or truck. They do not like to be filmed and discourage the use of cameras and taking photographs.

Schooling and Socializing

The traditional Amish schools are very simple, using one-room houses where only first to eighth grades are taught. Children only get education till the eighth grade, as Amish education after eighth grade is unnecessary to live an Amish lifestyle. Till eighth grade, the boys and girls get enough instruction to successfully perform their day-to-day duties.

Males are into farming and trading, and the women often perform household duties.

The Amish community is highly social, and the women meet quite often to quilt together, and perform other tasks together.

Clothing

The clothing is also a reflection of their faith, and the Amish faith is simple living. Males wear dark suits with pants, brown shoes for work, and black shoes casually. Amish men are also seen wearing hats. The hat's style shows the true reflection of the wearer's age. The Amish women wear full-skirted dresses in solid green, blue, brown, and orange. Instead of hats, they wear an apron and a cape, stockings, shawl, and a bonnet.

Barn-Raising Event

In the Amish community, a barn rising is an event in which barns are constructed. As the process requires labor, the entire community is called to take part in the construction. The volunteers perform the work and complete the barn in a matter of days.

The material for the barn is provided by families who need that barn. So, barn construction is a community effort. Men do the labor and women bring the food. Children learn and observe the process as they cannot participate.

Types of Food that Amish Can

The Amish do not eat meals consisting of noodles and pork that most Pennsylvania families eat. But the Amish families do incorporate Mexican and Italian meals into their diet.

For most of us, Amish canning seems to be a hobby rather than work, but the Amish people enjoy this task very much to prepare food for winter when their farms no longer give food. They feel proud of enjoying their harvest in the winter season, and for them, canning is a process of extending the life of their crops for the whole year.

The most common food that Amish families can eat includes soups, salsas, fruits, vegetables, and meat.

The top popular items that Amish can are listed below:

1. Chow Chow

A favorite canning item for Amish families is Chow Chow. It includes canning some delicious garden bounty into a glass jar. It is one of the specialties that the Amish love to preserve in jars.

2. Beets

The canned beets are one of the most typical items you can find sitting in their pantries. The canned beets are usually eaten at church meals.

3. Classic Favorite: Apple Butter

Apple butter is considered more like a condiment, used to spread over anything like bread.

4. Pickles & Relish

Pickles and relishes include pickled asparagus, pickled garlic, pickled beets, sweet garlic dill pickles, green tomato relish, pickled hot pepper, pickled snap peas, and much more.

5. Salsa

Salsa can be enjoyed with some tortilla chips or served with evening snacks. It is very settled taste with a mild spice kick, not too hot, not too plain. The Amish canning is not restricted to just meat and vegetables as you can fruit as well, just like a good, canned peach.

How the Amish Store Their Food

In the Amish community, it is the responsibility of women to safely store the surfeit of food. And as we told you earlier, the storage techniques have barely changed over the years and the same old techniques are passed on through generations. To prepare for the winter season, the Amish housewife usually preserves food and prepares dozens of cans and jars of fruits, vegetables, and meat.

Listed below are the methods used by the Amish for centuries to store their surplus food, of which the topmost is canning. So, now let us look into each of the techniques separately.

Canning

The food preservation through canning is almost completed in the Amish community as fall starts. The glass jars are used to preserve the food. These jars are scrubbed, washed, sterilized, and then filled with some delicious homemade recipes. Then, these jars are stored in kitchen pantries or shelves. Sauerkraut is one of the traditional Amish canned foods that is prepared by letting it ferment and stored in a crocks utensil holder for a week to ten days.

Cold Storage

We all know that Amish people are humble people who are far away from the comfort of modern days that we cannot even imagine living without. Still, a lot of Amish are quite modern and adopted few of these facilities. Thus, some of the Amish communities do allow the use of the freezer, still, the old school way is to stack large ice chunks into areas provided, known as a freezer. The lack of electricity leads to a simple lifestyle. In 1919, Amish leaders decided to permanently remove electricity. Some of the community also uses gas-powered generators and refrigerators at home.

Plentiful Food

The kitchen is the main hub, where all the family gathers and enjoys some delicious preserved and canned food that is kept stored throughout the year.

A Look Into Canning in Amish Communities and Their Traditions

To better understand the Amish canning, it is necessary to catch up with the traditions. Traditionally, canning is a duty performed by the women of the house, only when they are ready and serious about taking the duty of providing for and feeding their families. Usually, elder women of the house and children also help in the canning process.

For Amish women, it's not a duty, but a fun activity that includes the elders and children of the family, thus making it more of a festivity. Once the food canning is done, the joy and happiness that Amish women get just by looking into the jars is priceless, as they know they are all set for the winter season.

Amish women not only preserve fruits, pickles, and vegetables by using canning methods, but they also love to preserve meat, salsa, and soups which is not considered an easy task to do.

The chopping, food processing, and food preparation take a lot of time while canning salsa and soups.

All this work is done by hand and takes a lot of time, effort, love, and commitment. Canning provides the advantage of quickly serving the meal without the hustle of preparing, chopping, and cooking. Especially, the meat that is canned can be served and added right away to the dish being cooked.

Canning the meat is quick and easy compared to canning soup and salsa. Despite pressure canning the meat, Amish canning involves sealing the pre-cooked meat, or cooking meat, in the jar using a large boiling water pot for a few hours.

Amish canning does not require the food to be monitored. Amish canning allows a lot of techniques that the Amish community allows their women to adopt. Though the Amish follow the same old canning methods, still a lot of women can use generator-powered stoves as well. It's all depending on what their bishop allows them to adopt.

In today's modern society, a lot of Amish women use generator-powered stoves to heat water and sterilize their jars for canning food. Many Amish women use new lids with each jar, unlike any other method in which lids are boiled and reused.

Amish canning highly recommends using a new lid each time the meat is canned, as after doing so much hard work, you do not want to spoil the meat. The only means of preserving food is not limited to just canning the food, as a lot of Amish communities allow the women to use the freezer to store the food. Still, Amish people are highly connected to their roots, the majority of women prefer the canning method over freezing, and no doubt the frozen food tastes much different than canned food.

Canning surely needs commitment, time, and effort, but it is a very inexpensive method of storing food. You just need a few jars and kick-start the process of canning food. The canning of food in the Amish community is taken very seriously, and it's passed down from mother to daughter, from generation to generation.

Amish food is fantastic, and the Amish market sells authentic Amish canned food that includes fruit jams, preserves, vegetables, Chow Chow, and some other traditional delicacies. Authentic farmhouses also offer guides for canning techniques.

No doubt Amish canning provides a great deal, to store preserved food items that are enjoyed not only in winter, but throughout the year. Amish people are professional canners, especially when having large gardens, and a big family to feed. So, anyone can learn the Amish canning art, but it is necessary to prepare all the recipes correctly, following the National Center for Home Food Preservation guidelines.

2

Everything You Need To Know About Canning

If you are new to canning methods, then it is crucial to clarify the meaning of this term. Canning is a very fun technique for preserving food from spoiling by storing it in jars and containers that are sterilized and sealed by heat.

The invention of canning was not to answer the housekeeper's problems. But it was developed to answer the need to store food in such a way that it can be utilized further. In 1809, a researcher named Nicolas Appert invented this method. The reason behind this was the need to store the food that could be utilized by the army and navy.

History of Canning

In the late 1700s, during the war, Napoleon Bonaparte felt that his soldiers were not fed properly when they traveled long distances, far away from home. So, a very reliable method was searched for, that can keep the food safe for a longer period.

At that time, the government called for a person who could come up with an idea of storing and preserving food long term.

During that time, one chef, distiller, and candy maker named Nicolas Appert discovered that when the food is sealed in a jar and heat is applied to it, the food is preserved successfully.

So, in the 1800s, preserved food was practically consumed, as the army men, on their long travels, eat preserved meat, vegetables, milk, and fruits.

The preservation method of Nicolas', involved tightly sealing food inside a jar or a container and heating it for a specific time and maintaining that heat, leading to a seal that remained until the jar was reopened.

Still, it took about 50 years of research and study to finally get an answer as to why sealed food is not spoiled. And finally, Louis Pasteur explains that the growth of microorganisms is the basic cause of food spoilage. He further stated that canned food is safe to eat even after a year, as sealing the food keeps the food away from microorganism growth.

Then after several years, one Englishman named Peter Durand successfully created a method of sealing the food into tin-coated iron cans. And it was in 1813, that the first canning factory was established in England, which started canning food on a commercial basis.

At the start, these cans of food were very expensive, and out of reach for the average Joe. Until 1920, the main purpose of canning food was to serve the military personnel's needs.

After the 1920s, the canning caught on with housewives. To make the sealing process much easier, it was in 1882, when a lightning jar was introduced in markets.

The lightning jars had a glass lid and used a metal clamp to hold the lid and the gasket in place. This method was quite commonly used and manufactured in the USA and Europe. These lightning jars were very beautiful and produced in various sizes and shapes.

Then, Kerr jars and ball jars (1903) in the USA started manufacturing two pieces of rings and lids, which are still seen today. Nowadays, vegetables, meat, and fruits are stored in tin cans and soft drinks and many other beverages are stored in aluminum cans, as they are light and do not rust.

No doubt the canning process has revolved through these 200 years, and researchers and government agencies ensure the safety of food that has been canned, and these guidelines are updated as needed.

If you are interested in canning food or want to try any recipe that is handed over to you by your mother or grandmother, then it is best to look at the safest and most updated data. Still, you can use old-time recipes, with their own specific time and methods. Most of the time, it's been noticed that a lot of women are interested in the canning technique, but they have some doubts regarding its safety. Canning always follows precise methods, and you need to stick to them.
If you change up a recipe or add any other ingredients, then canned food ends up tasting awful.

It does not mean that one can't be creative and can't invent recipes, but it is necessary to first get comfortable with the process and educate oneself to the fullest. Even then, you should only make the changes once you are confident enough to do so. So, let us look into canning in much deeper terms.

Benefits of Canning

Canning has been a necessity of people since the beginning of time, as they need to preserve food. In today's modern society, where the day-to-day inflation and the rising cost of food affect the purchasing power, everyone looks for better and alternative ways to save some money on food, and canning is a great way to store some food and save money on purchasing highly priced items.

The canning process does require some effort, energy, and time, but it is worth it compared to going hungry in winter and buying expensive commercially canned food items.

Canning is inexpensive, safe, very popular, and a relatively simple method.

You can use this method to preserve sauces, pickles, soups, vegetables, and meat. The canning process helps kill the entire microorganism that causes illness or food spoilage. During canning when the jars are removed from the water bath, the air compresses and seals the food tightly with no contact with the outer world. This seal also protects the food from oxidation. Nowadays, we see dozens of canned foods lying on top of grocery store shelves. Still, canning is common in nearly every household, especially in the Amish community.

As the popularity of organic food is increasing, there is a need to preserve that organic food as well. Canning can be used to preserve our organic food domestically, packed up with social, economic, and health benefits. It is a safe, simple, effective, and inexpensive method, loaded with plenty of advantages. You just need to follow a research-based canning method to prevent food-borne illness.

Healthy

Canning is considered one of the healthiest methods of preserving food. It has numerous health benefits, especially when canning your organic crops. It ensures you have fresh and high-quality food, free from additives and preservatives.

Taste Packed Up With Quality

Your homemade, super delicious food can be preserved with fresh and locally grown ingredients. A store-packed food cannot beat the taste and quality of home-based canned food. You will always have various recipes packed up in cans and jars, stacked up in your kitchen pantry.

Economical

It is always expensive to buy commercially packed tin food. You can prepare that food for less than half the cost at home. Preparing the required food during the season and preserving it for future use saves you money and gives you a taste of your favorite food during the off-season. If you buy those items from the market, they would not taste the same and would also cost you more.

Practical Approach

People have always been worried about bad times and keep saving something for future use in the form of money or foodstuff. Food is a basic necessity and usually, during war times, there is no food available even if you have money. So canning food for uncertain times is more important than making a bomb shelter.

Preserve Harvest

If someone in your family is a farmer, and he has a garden of fruits or vegetables, you might have noticed that they preserve their extra harvest. Whenever harvest season comes, it is canned and saved for winter or even gifted to other family members. Jams can be made from freshly harvested fruits and can be used all year round. Canning the excess is a sensible way to avoid waste and enjoy it year-round.

Environmentally Friendly

Canning food at home is fuel-efficient; it might sound strange, but it saves countless miles that a factory-packed food travels; from the farm to the factory, then to the distributor, finally reaching the local store. It is also eco-friendly as it uses reusable or recycled jars, which we can repeatedly use to preserve different foods.

Economic Growth

Canning food domestically will also add to the economic growth of a country as it promotes local business. You can introduce your special recipes in your local market and earn plenty of profit with very little to no investment.

Affectionate Connection

Canning food and presenting it to your loved ones make your bond stronger with your relations. It was a habit of our mothers and grandmothers to make homemade jams and pickles and send them as gifts to their friends and family. The sentiments attached to the canned food are much more important than the food itself.

The Solution to the Power Outage

Most people prefer to preserve their food in the freezer because it's easy and convenient. But during power outages in extreme weather, frozen food can become stale or harmful by defrosting. Canning food is the best solution during such extreme weather.

Efficient Storage

There is always a limited space in your freezer to store food, but storage will never run out for your canned food. You can keep preserving and storing it on shelves, closets, storerooms, and even under your bed.

Cost Efficient

Canning food does not cost you much as you can use your old jars, rings, lids, and canners repeatedly for years. It is always recommended to sterilize the cans and jars before using them.

Know Your Food

Commercially canned food cannot contain the ingredients of your choice. Homemade organic canning lets you put exactly what you want in the can. Homemade canning does not contain artificial colors, chemical-based preservatives, high fructose syrups, or added flavoring.

Be a Proud Mother

Choose the best organic ingredients and preserve them for your family. Trust me; looking at the jars stored on your shelves gives you a sense of pride and accomplishment in feeding your family with the best healthy food.

Everyone knows that without freezers, we can't save our meat or dairy products. So, canning allows us to buy jars and save food like mangoes, okra, meat, tomatoes, fish, cabbage, and much more.

No doubt refrigerators are a great way to store and preserve food. Still, these technologies come with some side effects, thus some food tastes better canned than frozen.

Tools and Supplies Needed

Canning is no doubt a very effective way to increase the shelf life of food items. The food that is canned successfully with a proper seal lasts from one to five years. It depends upon the food group you are canning. If the canning is done according to set protocols and in the right circumstances, the canned food can also last much longer than five years. In 1974, one can of food was recovered from the wreck of Bertrand. It was about 109 years old and tested by the National Food Processors Association.

In history, canned food has always been a vital part of expeditions. In 1829, surgeon Edmund Rose took some canned food along with him to the Arctic. Canned food could stay and last for a longer period while keeping its edibility and nutrition.

When we talk about the tools and supplies that we need to make the food, the recipe is the most important thing that makes the foundation. A recipe allows canning to be safe and successful. Once you have a recipe book, you will have some great ideas on how to preserve the food properly from recipes that have already been tried and tested. You should look for the most authentic recipe from publications that are made by U.S Food and Agriculture departments. The major food processing equipment manufacturers also published some authentic information.

Along with the recipe and canner itself, there is also a lot of equipment you will need to ensure that your product is preserved properly.

Listed below are some tools and supplies that are 'must-haves' when canning any recipe:

- Long-handled spoon
- Measuring cup, usually large
- Timer or clock—needed for heat treatment times
- Lid wand
- Jar funnel
- Rubber spatula
- Water bath canner
- Jar rack
- 6–8-quart pot for boiling water
- Saucepan
- Canning jar
- Caps, lids, and screw bands
- Jar lifter
- Ladle for pouring recipes into the can

There are different styles of canning jars available on the market. The most-used jars nowadays are with two pieces of metal lid. The old-style jar comes with a wire bail, glass dome lids, and a rubber gasket.

It is recommended to use modern jars and new metal lids every time food is canned. The regular jars that are available in markets, and wide-mouth jars, are the best and work wonders for canning.

The regular jars are cheaper than wide-open jars, but wide-open jars are easy to fill.

So, if you are preparing larger food like whole vegetable pieces, or a large chunk of meat, then it is highly recommended to buy wide-mouth jars. It is very important to check for any crack in the body of the jar while buying or canning food. If the jar is not perfect, the seal won't be proper and the canning process would be a failure.

Usually, we have a lot of kitchen appliances and equipment that are already available.

Large Stock Pot

The large stock pots, or Dutch ovens, are quite handy when one decides to prepare recipes for canning and preserving. When it comes to canning, a bigger pot is better, as there is a lot of depth and surface area for the recipe and liquid to evaporate. The cast-iron heats quicker and cleaning up is very easy.

Chopstick

Once the recipes are poured into sterilized cans, then the chopstick becomes handy to stir the food like jams or jellies inside the jar to get rid of any air or bubbles.

A Kitchen Timer

It is a very handy tool that helps to follow the recipes time efficiently, to give some astonishing recipes and results. We all know cooking time is very crucial to make a perfect recipe.

Wooden Spoon

It helps to mix and stir jams, jellies, and salsa.

Mixing Bowls

The mixing bowls come in various sizes and help to hold fruits during the cutting and peeling process.

Sharp Knives

One should always have a pair of sharp knives to make chopping food easier. It also helps in peeling and chopping.

Tongs

During the canning process, the tongs serve as superman fingers that help reach hot areas without burning your own fingers. It becomes handy when taking out the lids from the stock pots.

Cheesecloth

It helps when someone is making jellies and jams.

How to Fit Canning into Your Life

Canning is a fairly easy process that can fit into anyone's daily routine. Canning is a very joyful activity for which you can find the time easily. If you are a stay-at-home wife, a mother, or if you are following a professional career, in all these cases you can base your wish of canning by motivating yourself and by being willing to give up a few of your activities to learn something new like canning.

Here are some guidelines to better fit canning into your life:

The most important thing is the willingness and the desire to learn. Here are just a few of the advantages to canning:

- Canning is an excellent way to give you food confidence that you cannot buy in any grocery store.
- Never add any artificial color, flavoring, or preservative to a home canned food, as home canning is all about plain, good, and nutritious food that is inside a jar.
- Always prepare the recipe at the home of which you are canning.
- Canned food is better than grocery-bought food because it is cooked by your own hands while watching and using the best available ingredients.
- Fitting canning into your lifestyle brings a lot of joy, as home-canned food items make great gifts.

- A person feels satisfaction knowing that the work of his hand is being appreciated and he can feed his family well.
- Instead of spending money on some entertainment like athletic events, concerts, and buying movie tickets, you can think of spending that money on learning canning techniques, which guarantees that your family eats clean and great food.
- By practicing canning you can also generate some great money at farmer markets by putting your canned food for sale.

Basics of Preservation

Preserving is a great way to save food for later use. If you fear that the food sitting in your pantry will spoil, then you can choose the food preservation process.

Food preservation helps to increase food life.

The preserving methods include freezing, canning, sugaring, salting, and refrigerating. Even vacuum packing is also a great way to preserve food. Food preservation is a method that is not new and has been around for centuries.

Preserving is no doubt a great way to retain the food quality while keeping it hygienic. Just the right set of protocols, tools, and equipment are needed to successfully preserve the food. Now, let us look into the importance of preserving food.

The Importance of Food Preservation

Preserving food is a great way to store food for the long term and minimize its shortage in the worst-case scenario.

It also helps in reducing the growth of pathogenic bacteria. We all know that food spoils easily, even stored in a pantry for a long time, due to bacteria like Ecolab, and salmonella. The bacteria need a warm and hot environment to grow and multiply rapidly. But the preservation process inhibits all those conditions that cause bacteria and food spoilage.

The food that is properly preserved keeps its taste, texture, and quality intact. As we all know, food is spoiled over time, and in many cases, spoiled food is unsafe to eat. That is not the case with food preservation.

The nutritional value of certain foods remains the same when food is preserved.

It also helps save you money in buying some unhealthy canned food items from grocery stores.

Methods of Food Preservation

Chilling

To chill the food, the appliance that we commonly use is a refrigerator. It is a great technology to freeze food at the lowest temperature. The method is very safe and adopted in every modern house, as a way to keep food fresh. The fridges have great technology to maintain the texture and quality of food, as it's cold, the bacteria growth is minimal.

Keynotes

- Set the temperature of the fridge between 1°C and 4°C.
- For commercial use, it should be less than 8°C.
- Use separate refrigerators for storing raw or ready-to-eat food, as it helps to prevent cross-contamination.
- You should teach yourself which shelf of the fridge is used for which specific item.
- Intact the labels of food and their expiry dates before storing them in the fridge.
- Do not overload the fridge.

Freezing

Frozen food lasts months if the right technique is applied to store the food. Bacteria cannot grow in a frozen environment and frozen food remains safe for a sufficient amount of time.
The food can be frozen for a few months to one year.

Keynotes

- The freezer temperature should be set between -18°C and -22°C.
- The food should be properly sealed and placed in air freezer bags. Proper wrapping is also an essential part when storing meat.
- It is not recommended to refreeze defrosted food, as it leads to bacterial growth.
- It is only recommended to freeze it for 24-hours and then utilize the defrosted food.
- It is important to defrost the freezer regularly to maximize its capabilities.
- Label food that you freeze.

Sugaring

The high sugar environment helps preserve food and stop bacteria growth, as the water content decreases. It is an effective way to make jams and marmalades. You can use the canning technique to store jams, jellies, and marmalades. Sugar granules, sugar syrup, or honey can be utilized for this purpose. Sugar is added to the recipe and sometimes even the use of alcohol alongside sugar is needed to preserve food.

Keynotes

- Fruits are preserved well with this technique.
- Vegetables like carrots, ginger, and relish are preserved by adding sugar.
- Fish and meat are preserved by adding them to brine made of sugar and salt.

Salting

It is a similar technique to sugaring as salt takes out the water from the food and stops the growth of bacteria. Too much salting may lead to food tasting unappetizing.

Keynotes

- Dry curing is a method of applying a dry salt rub to a vegetable or meat and leaving it to draw the water out.

- Wet curing is a method in which brine is prepared and then food is submerged in it, then it is preserved in cans to increase its shelf life.

Canning

As discussed earlier, canning is a great way to seal and pack the recipes, thus depriving the bacteria the oxygen they need to grow. It is a great way to increase the shelf life of food. The canning needs the right technique to kick start the process. The great thing about canning is that the recipe taste, texture, and color remain the same.

Vacuum Packing

It is quite similar to canning, the food lasts longer, and it also helps extend the shelf life of food. Vacuum packing creates a tight seal around food and deprives bacteria of oxygen. It is a great preserving technique that needs very little equipment and tools, unlike canning. It helps ensure optimum food quality.

Keynotes

- The recipes that need to be vacuumed should be prepared hygienically.
- Wash the fruits and vegetables well before vacuum sealing.
- It is necessary to cut any excess fat from the meat.
- Use a suitable plastic bag to vacuum seal the food.
- Use a vacuum packing machine to seal the food.
- Store the sealed bags in the fridge, or a cool dry place.
- Few vacuum sealing methods do not need machines to seal and pack the food. Still, there is always suitable equipment involved in the preservation method.

Types of Canning

Water Bath Canning

As the name indicates, jars of food are kept in fully covered, vigorously boiling water (as in a bathtub) for a prescribed amount of time. It is the easiest method of canning that helps you lock in the freshness of your homemade food for an entire year.

Required Supplies

Water bath canning does not require any specific appliances. You can use the supplies available in your home. So, it is not only the most accessible type of canning but also the cheapest.

You will need the following supplies for water bath canning:

- A sizable deep pot with a flat bottom usually made of aluminum, with a properly fitted lid. It should be large enough so that jars can submerge completely, leaving at least one inch above their top.
- A rack that can fit inside the canner to keep the jars elevated above heat. If you place the jars on the bottom of the pot, direct heat can cause cracks in them.
- Proper canning jars with clean, rust-free metal bands.
- Metal canning lids that fit your jars. Use a new lid every time you process your food.
- Canning funnel, preferably made of stainless steel or plastic. It will save your food from spilling onto the rim of the jar.
- A jar lifter.

Suitable Foods

Water bath canning is only suitable for high-acid food, like tomatoes, berries, fruits, and pickled vegetables. It is ideal for making jams, jellies, salsa, fruits, and pickles. Their natural acidity helps them to preserve safely without the use of pressure. Water bath canning can only heat foods until boiling point, i.e., 212°F/100°C. However, low acid food requires higher temperatures around 241°F/116°C to kill harmful bacteria adequately.

Note: High acid foods are foods that have a pH level reading of 4.6 or lower.

Water Bath Canning Step By Step

Here is the step-by-step process for water bath canning. Before starting the process, have your supplies ready. Properly sterilize the jars, lids, and bands in a dishwasher or wash in soapy hot water.

Common Equipment for Water Bath Canning

- Water bath canner
- Jar rack
- 6 (or larger) quart pot for boiling water
- Saucepan
- Canning jar
- Caps lids and screw bands
- Jar lifter
- Funnel

- Spatula/Spoons
- Ladle for pouring recipes into the can

Altitude Adjustment Chart

- 1,001-3,000 feet—increase by 5 minutes
- 3,001-6,000 feet—increase by 10 minutes
- 6,001-8,000 feet—increase by 15 minutes
- 8,001-10,000 feet—increase by 20 minutes

Notes

- Wash all your equipment with soapy warm water and rinse under tap water.
- Fill the water bath canner with water halfway up.
- Let the water get hot.
- Avoid boiling water.
- Now, adjust cans into the jar rack and place the jar rack inside the water bath canner.
- Let it sit inside for ten minutes.
- Add the lids to a separate pot with hot water so the lids submerge.
- Let the lids also simmer for a few minutes.
- Take out the lids and canning jars, the canning jars are ready to use.
- Now fill the jars, by leaving a little space on top, and close the lid.
- Place the jar rack inside the canning pot and pour water in it and let the water come to a boil.

Note: for raw packed jars, have the water in the canners hot, not boiling, to prevent breakage of the jar. For hot-packed jars, use hot or gently boiled water. Once the water comes to a boil and a required temperature is reached, use the tongs to put the jars inside the pot, if necessary, pour more water, as it should be covered with 1-inch of boiling water from the top.

Then start the timer for the correct processing time. The processing time depends on what you are preserving, the altitude, and whether you are hot packing or raw packing. Once the time limit is reached, switch off the burner and take off the lid. Let the jars stay inside the water for five minutes. Now lift them with a canning tong. Leave the jars on a dry surface for almost 24-hours. Next, you need to check the tightness of the lids, clean them with a dry towel, label them with the recipe, time, or date, and store them in a cool and dry place.

Pressure Canning

Some foods need to be processed at high temperatures; pressure canning is the most suitable method for such foods. You can use this process with low-acid foods like meats, soups, and vegetables; high-acid foods can go stale using this method. It is not much different from water bath canning, but the appliance is different.

Suitable appliance

You are mistaken if you are using a traditional pressure cooker to do pressure canning. Temperature cannot be adequately controlled in conventional cookers, and they also fail to distribute heat evenly, which is necessary to kill the stubborn bacteria. So, it would be best if you had a good pressure canner for this purpose.

A pressure canner consists of three main parts, a large pot, and a lid that locks on the pot, and a dial or weighted gauge. The gauge that is used on the top of the pressure canner works as a regulator that makes a proper steam pressure. It can make up to 240°F steam with just two to three inches of water.

Pressure Canner Regulators

All pressure canners have a dial, or a knob-like device, called pressure regulators. It helps in controlling the pressure inside the canner. Three types of pressure canners or pressure canner regulators are available on the market.

1. Dial Gauge Regulator

More common in older pressure canners, a dial gauge regulator indicates the pressure and heat inside the canner through a dial placed on top of the appliance. As the heat and pressure increase, the dial rises. It is necessary to monitor the gauge and adjust the heat when it is in use to maintain the correct pressure. Dial gauge pressure can be adjusted for higher altitudes. For instance, if the altitude is 2000 feet or below, the pressure should be 11 pounds for meat and vegetables, and 6 pounds for fruits.
Note: a dial gauge regulator must be inspected for accuracy annually.

2. Weighted Gauge Regulator

The weighted gauge pressure canner has a disc-like piece of metal, which is set on the vent pipe to control the pressure. The pressure level is indicated through 5, 10, and 15-pound markings. It makes a rocking sound when it reaches the required pressure. Some weights jiggle three or four times a minute; others jiggle continuously. Start monitoring your pressure after it starts jiggling. Meat and vegetables require 10 pounds of pressure and fruits require 5 pounds.
Note: altitude above 1000 feet needs an increase of five more pounds to the pressure.

3. One-Piece Regulator

A one-piece pressure regulator is the most common type available in the market. It consists of three metal rings that can be added or removed to adjust the pressure canner for 5, 10, or 15 pounds. Each additional metal ring adds 5 pounds to the pressure. First, set the regulator on the top of the vent pipe, and then start the pressurizing process. The rattling sound of the regulator will help you to adjust the heat.

4. Suitable Foods

Pressure canning produces pressure and a lot of heat; it is not suitable for many food items like sweet and salty food items and epically acidic foods. The heat and pressure cause these types of food to get mushy, lose their texture, and become hard. The acidic element of some foods can be reduced by combining them with other foods. When you cook non-acidic food with acidic food, it somewhat balances out the acid enough to have a successful pressure canning. Some fruits are acidic when unripe and less acidic when ripe. It is advised to check the acidity of food items using a pH strip or pH meter before pressure canning.

Note: foods that have a pH greater than 4.6 are suitable for pressure canning.

Pressure Canning Step-By-Step

- Heat the jar for a few minutes to sterilize.
- Fill hot jars with recipes and pack them tightly.
- Remove air bubbles; you can use a spatula for this purpose.
- Clean the jar rim, set the lid in place, and screw the band on tightly.
- Set all the jars in the canner.
- Then lock the lid.
- Make sure that water covers only a few inches and that jars are not submerged in water.
- Turn the flame to high and let the steam escape the vent pipe for about 10–12 minutes, then put on the pressure regulator.
- Once the pressure regulator starts, adjust the heat.
- Once the required time is up, depressurize the canner before opening.
- Wait for ten minutes, and then remove the jars from the canner. Let them cool for 12–24 minutes before storing.

Atmospheric Steam Canning

Atmospheric steam canning is the most modern and scientifically approved method of preserving homemade food. In this method, the heat of steam is used to preserve food. This steam atmosphere gets to 100°C, so we have the same sterilizing heat available as when we boil water. It sounds similar to water bath canning, but steam canning saves water, energy, and time; they do not boil over.

Suitable Appliance

Atmospheric steam canners consist of a shallow pan, a fitted rack, and a high dome cover. It is designed to trap steam and gradually release it in a very controlled fashion. It is different from pressure canners which is why it is labeled as an atmospheric steam canner or steam canner, to differentiate it from pressure canners, which also use steam.

Suitable Food

This method is used for naturally acidic or properly acidified food. This method can preserve jams, jellies, most fruits, pickles, relishes, chutneys, salsa, and tomato products. The same food or recipes used for water bath canning can be used here. It is an alternative or modern version of water bath canning.

Atmospheric Steam Canning Step-by-Step

- Put the required amount of water in the atmospheric steam canner, as recommended by the manufacturer.
- Add a few drops of vinegar; this will prevent the jar outside from becoming cloudy.
- Put the rack into the canner and switch on the burner. You can put the lid on the pot to preheat quickly.
- Remove the lid after ten minutes and place the jars in the racks.
- Put the lid back on and wait for the steam to reach maximum temperature.
- Now note the time and put the burner heat on low to maintain the full head of steam.
- Let the canner steam for the prescribed time. Please do not lift the lid off as we do not want to break the cycle of the steaming process.
- When the time is up, turn off the burner and wait for five minutes.
- Remove the jars with a tong or kitchen mitts.
- Let them stand on a clean surface for 12–24 hours before storing.

Acidity in Food

As we have discussed earlier in types of canning, certain food requires a certain type of canning method to preserve the food. If high acidic food is canned using pressure canning, it would be a great disaster.

Thus, we can say that the pH level of food plays a huge role in deciding which method is needed for food canning.

- The acidic food releases hydrogen ions, which gives it a sour taste.
- The pH range is between 0–14.
- A pH of 7 is neutral; pure water has a pH of 7.
- The values greater than 7 are alkaline and values less the 7 are acidic.
- The high acidic food has a range below 7.
- When we decide on food canning, the pH level of food is a great determining factor in this overall process.
- Food that is considered acidic, like berries and pickles can be canned using the water bath canning method.
- Alkaline food can be canned using pressure canning.
- All the green leafy vegetables and meat with pH above 4.6 are canned using a pressure canning method.

The bacteria named Clostridium is behind the science of choosing the canning method. To prevent this bacterium from growing, low acidic food must be canned using pressure canning. This bacterium can easily be grown in a sealed jar with a low heat or low temperature. So, pressure canning is applied to kill this bacterium, as we know the temperate is 240–250°C in pressure canning.

Some foods that have a pH of 4.6 or above, like tomatoes and figs, can be water bath canned, while considered to be acidic food because we mix lemon juice or citric acid into the recipes to make it safe to use water bath canning.

Water Bath Canning or Pressure Canning: Which One to Choose

While learning about both the canning processes, you will find out that they are not at all complicated.

As we have already looked in detail at both canning processes, so we will wrap up by discussing which of the methods is the best to preserve the food.

Canning is a very simple method that calls for boiling the jars and sterilizing them so that we can put recipes in them for preservation.

Pressure canning is also similar to water bath canning, but it is more of an intense process, as we are putting the jars and contents under high pressure.

Pressure canning is more expensive than water bath canning, and it also requires more moving parts.

If you are a beginner, then you will be intimidated thinking about them exploding when using the pressure canning. For some of the beginners, the fear is even worse.

Water bath canning mainly focuses on heating things to sterilize them. This process is simple and much faster than pressure canning. It usually takes 10 to 15 minutes for a recipe in a water bath to process. And it takes less than an hour to make a recipe and fill the jars until it is completely done.

With water bath canning, you can only preserve the foods that are high in acid. As acidic food is naturally resistant to bacteria and bacteria have a hard time growing in the sealed environment. For high acidic food, you let the jars stay in the water bath canners for a much longer time.

The pressure canning is for all those food items that are low in acid. For example, meat should always be pressure canned. Even if the meat is cooked, it still needs a pressure can.

So, both of the methods are best on their own, while preparing versatile recipes. You cannot choose water bath canning for low acidic food, and for higher acidic food you cannot use pressure canning.

Here's a small list to give you an idea of which is best for which food item:

Water Bath Canning

- Fruits and fruit juices
- Salsas
- Jams and jellies
- Pickled food
- Relish

Pressure Canning

- Meat
- Potatoes

- Carrots
- Green beans (any bean, really)
- Peas
- Anything with meat

The proper required processing methods to can low and high acidic foods

When bacteria is grown in canned food it can turn deadly and cause botulism. It may lead to severe food poisoning. These harmful bacteria actually exist as vegetative or spore cells. These cells can easily survive in water and in the ground for several years and once the conditions are favorable, these grow to vegetative cells. This cell multiplies rapidly and creates deadly toxins within a matter of days.

The ideal environment consists of the following:

- Have a very moist environment with low-acid food.
- Having a temperature range between 40°F and 120°F.
- Having no greater than two percent oxygen.

The surfaces they reside in are usually fresh food items.

There are many bacteria and molds that are not easy to remove from the surface of the food. Washing can remove the numbers, but it does not kill all the bacteria. Peeling the roots or blanching can also help, but the most successful means to remove these bacteria are applying canning techniques.

Food Acidity and The Ways to Process

The control of bacterial growth in both canning methods is based on the food pH level. The pH determines the acidity of food. The acidity can be natural, as in most fruits. The low-acid canned food is not acidic enough to reduce or eradicate the growth of the bacteria. High acidic food has enough acidity to prevent the bacteria growth. If you are water bath canning the low acid food, its acidity can be increased by adding vinegar, lemon juice, or even citric acid. Low-acid foods like meat, fish, poultry, milk, and vegetables except tomatoes can be water bath canned by adding a good amount of acid like lemon juice or vinegar to it.

The bacteria Botulinum is more easily destroyed at higher temperatures. So, the low-acid foods have a range to sterilize at 240°F to 250°F, this is possible with pressure canners that are operated at 10 to 15 pounds per square inch of pressure. The time ranges from 20–100 minutes.

The time depends on the type of food, the jar size, and the way it's packed in the jar.

Canned Foods (Special Diets)

Products like baby food and canned food without sugar often cost a huge amount which prompts interest in home canning these special items.

The low sugar, low salt, and baby food can easily be canned at home, and it is a safe method as well.

For canning the fruits and other items without sugar, it is crucial to select the full ripe food that is the best quality. Mostly, the low-sugar fruits are prepared in hot packs and can be used in water or fruit juice instead of sugary syrup. Fruit juices of the same fruit that is being canned is the best solution available. Splenda is the best substitute for canning fruits.

Canning (reduced sodium): the salt seasons the ingredients, but it is not necessary. A lot of recipes that are canned in this book use no salt.

Can You Reuse Canning Lids?

The canning lids are great tools to seal the jars properly. Reusing them is not a great idea. Using the canning lids more than once can result in the jars not being sealed properly. The canning lid has a sealing compound around the rim that is only good for one-time use. So, if you want canning work done properly, then it is recommended to use new canning lids. An attempt to save a few dollars in return on rotten canned food is not a good idea, as canning lids are not at all expensive, so risking your health isn't worth that small amount.

You might be wondering why there is no means to reuse the canning lid, but here is the good news: replacing your canning lids does not mean that you need to throw the old ones away.

The old lids can be used to store dried goods, salad dressing, and other non-canned food items. Moreover, if it is a pain for you to buy new canning lids each year, then switch to reusable canning lids. The reusable canning lids are designed to be used over and over again and they are safe for both water bath canning and pressure canning. But if the reusable canning lid becomes cracked or chipped then it will not create a good seal, only then it is not recommended to use them.

The reusable lids cost more than the regular canning lids. But if you love canning and you are into canning a lot, then you can make a purchase and do a one-time investment to buy reusable lids to save some money over and over again.

Ways to Save On Canning Lids

You can stock up on canning lids when they're on sale and save money. It's recommended not to buy too many lids, as the rubber seal dries out over time.

So, if you do canning in bulk, then buy the lids in bulk as well. Online retailers have some great deals, and they are a great source to save money.

As you cannot reuse metal canning lids, you can reuse the jars and band until they are no longer in good condition.

How to Spot a Canned Good That Has Expired

Many times, we come across the canned food sitting in the kitchen pantries, which are several years old. Despite thinking of utilizing them or not, those canned items need to be tossed out. When home canning the food, the canned food does not have an expiry date or any label.

But what about cans that pass their 'use by' dates by a few weeks, months, or even years? Here are some guidelines for what to toss and what to keep.

The canned food purchased from grocery stores have a 'use by' label or 'best before.' They do not have an expiry date. These dates are labeled by manufacturers. The 'best by' date is the time to use the product for the best physical or sensory quality.

The 'use by' is the date till the product will be at its peak quality in terms of freshness. As we know that canning is a process of heating the food and sealing it in a way that the bacteria could not reach it. Thus, it is safe for a longer period and even for 7–8 years.

So, what about the labeled dates provided on canned food. After the best by date, the quality of food degrades, but still, the food is edible and does not contain harmful toxins.

The canned food is sealed and vacuumed, which protects it from light, so the freshness remains intact. If you are interested in spotting bad canned food, then first look for the physical appearance of canned food; if it is leaking, rusted, or has a deep dent then you should not buy or consume the canned food. The canned food should always be placed in a cool and dark area. If the canned food is sitting under a temperature of 85°F, then it's fine, however more than 100°F is not ideal for canned food items.

If the canned food is exposed to light for a longer time, then it should not be consumed. It is highly recommended to check home-canned food for good shape.

There is not just one, but several conditions and circumstances that can affect the quality of your canned food, but still, the foods are usually not considered harmful or dangerous. The one major detector of rotten food is discoloration. Keep in mind that certain food changes their color with time. It is very crucial to understand which food has been spoiled and which has not.

Below are some common conditions that you might face when doing home canning. The first is the loss of liquid content from the canned food before or after processing the jars. This happens because the jars are not sealed tightly, the rapid fluctuation of pressure in the canner, or the bubbles are not removed after pouring recipes into the jars. If you are using a water bath canning technique, then in the water bath canner the level of the water perhaps dropped below the jars.

Sometimes, you will encounter some dark food at the top of the canning jars, which happens when the packing and the processing instructions are not followed properly. Most of the fruits and vegetables float in jars when you haven't used enough sugar or sugar syrup, as the fruit itself is lighter than the sugar syrup.

Few vegetables turn black, it happens because water with too much iron is used to process the food. We highly recommend discarding all the black vegetables and fruit as it is a true indicator of food spoilage.

Sometimes, a person encounters vegetables, especially beets, that turn very light or white, it happens when the beets are not fresh, making canning an unsuccessful process.

Sometimes, preserved vegetables turn brown, the brown color is not an indicator of food spoilage, but still, for many, it is not attractive to eat. Vegetables also turn brown and olive green because of the breakdown of chlorophyll in the food, overcooking the recipe, or canning mature vegetables. Still, it's considered safe to eat.

Sometimes, yellow crystals form inside canned food, especially in green vegetables that are formed naturally because of the release of glycoside in the vegetables; it is also safe to eat.

Many times, white segments settle down into the jars. It indicates that the starch in the food items has settled on the bottom of the jar, as hard water was used to process the food. It is usually considered safe to eat.

If the food is cloudy and soft, it indicates bacterial spoilage, the food is considered not safe to eat.

Sometimes, food turns blue, pink, purple, or red, this color is generated because of the natural chemical change of the fruits and vegetables like apples, pears, and peaches. The food is safe to eat.

You prepared jelly and it is moldy, which indicates an improper seal. That food is not safe to eat. It is highly recommended to remove all the bubbles from the jelly after pouring the jelly into the jar.

Talking about canning meat or seafood, you often see some fish worms, because the fish is held too long before processing, which lowers the quality of the food.

We highly recommended avoiding iodized salt when canning meat items like chicken, turkey, or tuna.
It is encouraged to use your doubts. If you are doubtful enough, you can throw the food.

Basic Tips for Success

The first step is to take the entire appliance for a spin by checking all the necessary equipment for quality. For example, the sealing gaskets need to be checked to make sure that they seal properly.
If you are using pressure canning, then it is also necessary to check the pressure display of dial gauges.
Following the recipe is the very first step in making food preservation through canning successful. You should have all the necessary equipment and tools that are needed for canning. Shop for the entire ingredients ahead. It is recommended to follow the recipe direction and size for a prompt cooking and canning experience.

The jars need to be sterilized properly and before that, you should look for any dents or cracks. The jar rack and jar lifter always become handy, when taken out and submerging jars into the water to process.

The jar's position should always be upright, so it prevents spillage..

In pressure canning, less water is needed as compared to water bath canning. If the recipe did not mention the amount of water, then enough water should be added to have a level of 2–3 inches in the kettle.

You should always be precise with the timing of processing the cans. In pressure canning, start the processing timer once the dial gauge shows that it's reached the recommended pressure. If the pressure drops, then bring it back to the desired temperature and start the processing time. You need to adjust the recipes processing time, according to the altitude level.

In pressure canning, it is always recommended to turn the heat off after the processing time completes. And then turn off the flame, and let it cool off naturally. And once the kettle has cooled off, completely remove the weights from the vent pipes and again, wait a few minutes to close the lid and remove the lid carefully, so that the direct steam is away from your face, use a shield for that if you have one available.

In water bath canning, carefully lift the jars from the canner or large stockpots. The jars should always be upright. Store the jars after letting them cool for 24-hours in a cool and dark place.

It's always recommended to prepare bigger batches as it saves time and effort. Choose organic, fresh fruits, vegetables, and other ingredients.

3

General Canning Guidelines

Canning is a great and economical way to preserve the food that your family loves to eat all year long.

Here are some general guidelines for canning food:

- It is recommended to adjust the processing time at higher altitudes; if you live at 1000ft above sea level, then processing food at sea level would lead to bacterial growth.
- Microwave ovens and dishwashers are not recommended to process the freshly filled jars.
- The open kettle canning technique should also not be practiced.
- The food's freshness and wholesomeness should be ensured to prepare recipes for canning.
- To maintain the natural texture, color, and quality of canned food, it is recommended to use high-quality, fresh, and seasoned fruits and vegetables that are properly mature and free from disease.
- Can the recipe as quickly as it is prepared.
- Make a solution: take 20 cups of water and mix it with 3 grams of ascorbic acid and keep the peeled and diced fruits and vegetables in this solution while preparing the canner load for jars. It helps in keeping the color and texture of food.
- Sterilize the jars properly.
- Pour or dump the foods into jars, then adjust the headspace that should be about 1–1.4 inch (defined in the recipes).
- Screw the bands tightly and securely.
- After processing the jars, let them cool at room temperature.
- Test the jar seal by pressing the lid on the center with a finger. If the lid comes back up with the release of your finger, the lid is unsealed. So, you need to reprocess the jar, for that, open the jar to check for tiny nicks or you can also use a new jar and start the canning process fresh.
- Store and place the jars in a cool, dark place. The temperature should be between 50°F and 70°F.
- Always select the exact processing time.

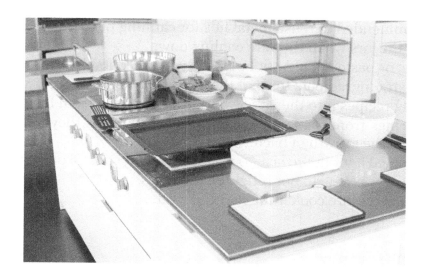

Dos and Don'ts of Home Canning

Home canning is a technique that needs practice to make it successful. When home canning food, ensure all the steps are followed, as these steps help to keep the quality of canned food.

- Sterilize the canning jars properly.
- Buy all the necessary ingredients and assemble all the equipment ahead.
- Canning is a science, and it does not have to be rushed, so give canning proper time.
- Always use new jar lids, as if the lid is used multiple times, the rubber seal on the jar is thin, and its exposure to heat breaks down the seal. Using lids more than once causes food spoilage.
- Use the recipes only from authentic sources.
- Find the recipes that are following USDA guidelines.
- Recipe ingredients should be as natural as possible.
- Make sure that the low acid food recipes are canned properly.
- Use the jars that are manufactured for canning purposes like Ball or Kerr jars. As these jars can withstand the heat and high temperatures, other jars would not stand.
- The canned food that is prepared commercially uses a different method than home canning, and the jars are used for one-time purposes, so the jars are not designed for repeat canning. So, do not put any canned ingredients purchased from the grocery store into our home-canned recipes.
- Store the high acid food using water bath canning.
- Low acidic food must be processed using pressure canning.
- It is not recommended to use the canning method for dairy products.
- Choose canning recipes from the National Center for Home Food Preservation, as the recipes are tested for safety.
- It is recommended to label and date the canned jars before storing them.
- It is necessary to make altitude adjustments.
- Discard the jars that are cracked or have an imperfect seal.
- We do not recommend trying recipes published before 2009, even from authentic sources.

- Understand the science behind the canning and update your knowledge.
- It is not recommended to reuse metal lids for canning purposes.
- Do not cover the jars when they are cooling down.
- Rice, noodles, or pasta should not be added to canned food.
- Do not add extra ingredients to what the specific recipes call for.
- When pouring recipes into the jars always leave 1/4-inch from the top of the jar.
- Remove the rings from the jars before storing the jars, as they might not have sealed and this can lead to the growth of bacteria.
- Food has changed a lot in the last 50 years, so do not stick to old canning techniques.
- After jars are processed, do not retighten the rings.
- Do not use the pressure cooker for canning food.

4

Recipes

Note 1: Sterilization of Canning Jar (Empty)

While preserving the jellies, spreads, jams, and pickled products, the items that are processed for no more than ten minutes should be filled into sterilized canning jars. To sterilize these canning jars after washing with warm soapy water and rinsing thoroughly, you need to dump these jars into a water bath canner by adjusting all the jars in the canning rack.

Fill the water bath canner with 1–2 inches of water, then submerge the jar rack with jars, and let it boil for ten minutes at an altitude less than 1000ft and add one minute with each additional 1000ft elevations.

Reduce the flame and let the jars stay underwater. Remove the jars one at a time and then fill the jars with the prepared recipes. The canning jars that are used to fill recipes in a pressure canner do not need to be pre-sterilized.

Note 2: Preparing and Using the Syrups

Once the fruits are canned, adding fruit juice or syrup to it helps it to retain texture and flavor. It also helps to eliminate the growth of harmful bacteria and food spoilage. The guide below will help you to prepare syrup for any fruit:

Syrup Type	Approximate % Sugar	For 9 Quart		For 7 Quart Load		Fruits Packed In Syrup
		Water Cups	Sugar Cups	Water Cups	Sugar Cups	
Very Light	10	6-1/2	3/4	10	1-1/4	Natural Sugar Levels
Light	20	5-3/4	1-1/2	9-2/4	2-1/4	Very Sweet Fruit
Medium	30	5-1/4	2-1/4	8-1/4	3-3/4	Sweet Fruits Like Sweet Apples Cherries
Heavy	40	5	3-1/4	7-3/4	5-1/4	Tart Fruits Like Apples, Cherries, Gooseberry
Very Heavy	50	4-1/4	4-1/4	6-1/2	6-3/4	Very Sour Fruits

Category: Fruit and Pie Fillings

Apple Pie Filling

Yield: 7 quarts

Ingredients:

6-quart Rome apples, sliced
5-1/2 cups of white granulated sugar
1.5 cup of clear gel
2.5 cups of cold water
1 teaspoon of cinnamon
5 cups apple juice
¾ cup lemon juice

Directions:

1. First wash, peel, and core all the apples.
2. Then slice the apples about half an inch.
3. Add the apple slices to water containing ascorbic acid solution (3 grams of ascorbic acid into 1 gallon of cold water) to prevent the apples from getting brown.
4. Now add about 6 cups of apple per 1 gallon of boiling water in a large pot.
5. Work in batches for this step.
6. Boil for 1 minute (each batch), after water returns to a boil, and then drain apple slices, and keep heated fruit in a covered bowl or any large stock pot.
7. Next mix the clear gel, sugar, and cinnamon in a kettle and pour on apple juice and cold water.
8. Cook on medium until it starts to bubble.
9. Add the lemon juice and cook for 1 more minute.
10. Add in the drained apples and then fill the hot, sterilized jars with the mixture as quickly as possible leaving 1-inch of headspace.
11. Remove any air bubbles and then clean the rims of jars.
12. Adjust the lid and process immediately.
Note: if apples are less tart in taste, add ¼ cup of lemon to this recipe.

Recommended processing time in a boiling-water canner:

Style Of Pack	Jar Size	0-1000 Ft	1001-3000ft	3001-6000ft	Above 6000
Hot	Pint Or Quarts	25 Minutes	30 Minutes	35 Minutes	40 Minutes

Blueberry Pie Filling

Yield: 7 quarts

Ingredients:

6 quarts blueberries
6 cups granulated sugar
½ cup lemon juice
2 cups clear gel
7 cups of cold water

Directions:

1. The first step is to wash the blueberries.
2. Pour 1 gallon of water into a large kettle.
3. Let it boil on high until it begins to bubble.
4. Pour about 6 cups of blueberries into 1 gallon of water and work in a batch; let it boil for 1 minute.
5. Then drain the berries and keep the heated fruit in a covered bowl or any large stock pot.
6. Take a large kettle and add sugar and clear gel.
7. Pour in the water and let it cook until thickened.
8. Keep stirring and add lemon juice, boil it for 1 more minute.
9. Add the drained berries immediately to the hot, sterilized jars with the mixture as quickly as possible leaving 1-inch of headspace.
10. Remove any air bubbles and then clean the rims of jars.
11. Adjust the lid and process immediately.

Recommended processing time in a boiling-water canner:

Style Of Pack	Jar Size	0-1000 Ft	1001-300 oft	3001-600 oft	Above 6000
Hot	Pint Or Quarts	30 Minutes	35 Minutes	40 Minutes	45 Minutes

Mixed Fruit Cocktail

Yield: 5–6 pints

Ingredients:

3 pounds of peaches
3 pounds of pears
1.5 pounds seedless green grapes, under-ripe
3 cups white sugar
4 cups water

Directions:

1. Wash the grapes and then add them to the ascorbic acid solution (3 grams of ascorbic acid into 1 gallon of cold water).
2. Now add the peaches into boiling water for 1 minute.
3. Once the skin loosens, add it to the cold water.
4. Cut and remove the pit after discarding the skin.
5. Add it to the grape solution.
6. Now, cut the peel, and core the pears.
7. Add it to the solution with grapes.
8. Take a saucepan and combine water and sugar.
9. Boil it and then add drained fruits from the solution into the boiling water.
10. Let it boil.(See the recommended boiling time)
11. Then add this fruit mixture to the jars.
12. Add ½ cup of liquid to each jar with fruit chunks.
13. Leave about ½-inch head space.
14. Remove any air bubbles.
15. Clean the rims of the jars.
16. Adjust the lids onto the jars and then process.

Recommended processing time in a boiling-water canner:

Style Of Pack	Jar Size	0-100 0 Ft	1001-300 oft	3001-60 ooft	Above 6000
Raw	Half Pint Or Pint	20 Minutes	25 Minutes	30 Minutes	35 Minutes

Berry Syrup

Yield: About 8–9 half-pints

Ingredients:

6.5 cups of fresh strawberries
6-3/4 cups of white sugar

Directions:

1. Wash the berries and then remove the caps.
2. Crush the berries in the saucepan.
3. Cook it until it boils and then simmer for about 10 minutes.
4. Strain this mixture through a colander and drain as much liquid from the pulp.
5. Pass this mixture through a cheesecloth into a bowl.
6. Discard the leftover pulp.
7. This will yield 5 cups.
8. Combine it with sugar in a kettle or a saucepan.
9. Bring this mixture to a boil and collect any scum from on top.
10. Next, fill this mixture into half a pint or pint jars, leaving about ½-inch of headspace.
11. Do remember to remove the air bubbles and then clean the rim and adjust the lid and process quickly.

Recommended processing time in a boiling-water canner:

Style Of Pack	Jar Size	0-1000ft	1001-6000 ft	Above 6000ft
Hot	Half Pint Or Full Pints	10 Minutes	16 Minutes	20 Minutes

Processing directions for canning strawberries in a dial, or weighted-gauge canner, is listed in tables 1 and 2.

Table 1
Processing times for some acidic foods in a weighted-gauge pressure canner:

Type Of Fruits	Style Of Pack	Size Of Jars	Process Time	PSI At Altitude	
				0-1000ft	Above 1000ft
Apple	Hot	Pints Or Quarts	8	5 Pounds	10 Pounds
Berries	Hot And Raw (Pints Only)	Pints Or Quarts	8	5 Pounds	10 Pounds
Berries	Raw	Quarts	10	5 Pounds	10 Pounds
Cherries Sweet And Sour	Hot	Pints	8	5 Pounds	10 Pounds
Cherries Sweet And Sour	Hot	Quarts	10	5 Pounds	10 Pounds
Cherries Sweet And Sour	Raw	Pints Or Quarts	10	5 Pounds	10 Pounds
Peach, Apricots	Hot And Raw	Pints Or Quarts	10	5 Pounds	10 Pounds
Pear	Hot	Pints Or Quarts	10	5 Pounds	10 Pounds
Plum	Hot And Raw	Pints Or Quarts	10	5 Pounds	10 Pounds

Table 2

Processing times for some acidic foods in a dial-gauge pressure canner:

Type Of Fruits	Style Of Pack	Size Of Jars	Process Time	PSI At Altitude			
				0-2000ft	2001-4000ft	4001-6000ft	6001-8000ft
Apple	Hot	Pints Or Quarts	8	6	7	8	9
Berries	Hot	Pints Or Quarts	8	6	7	8	9
Berries	Raw	Pint	8	6	7	8	9
Berries	Raw	Quarts	10	6	7	8	9
Cherries Sweet And Sour	Hot	Pints	8	6	7	8	9
Cherries Sweet And Sour	Hot	Quarts	10	6	7	8	9
Cherries Sweet And Sour	Raw	Pints Or Quarts	10	6	7	8	9
Peach, Apricots	Hot And Raw	Pints Or Quarts	10	6	7	8	9
Pear	Hot	Pints Or Quarts	10	6	7	8	9
Plum	Hot And Raw	Pints Or Quarts	8	6	7	8	9

Category: Vegetables

Spinach

Ingredients:

28 pounds of spinach is needed per canner load of 7 quarts
An average of 18 pounds is needed per canner load of 9 pints

Notes:

Discard any discolored, wilted, or damaged leaves.
Use fresh and attractive leaves that are bright in color.

Directions:

1. Wash the greens and drain the water.
2. Clean all the dust and grits.
3. Cut the stems.
4. Add about 1 pound of greens at a time in cheesecloth and blanch in a steamer basket for 5 minutes, once wilted, set aside.
5. Repeat the process in batches for all the greens.
6. Fill the jars loosely with greens and add on top the boiling water, leaving about 1-inch of headspace. Remove air bubbles.
7. Clean the rims of the jars.
8. Adjust the lids onto the jars and then process.

Recommended processing time in a dial-gauge pressure canner:

			PSI At Altitude			
Style Of Pack	Size Of Jars	Processing Time	0-2000ft	2001-4000ft	4001-6000ft	6000-8000ft
Hot	Pints	70 Minutes	11 Pounds	12 Pounds	13 Pounds	14 Pounds
	Quarts	90 Minutes	11 Pounds	12 Pounds	13 Pounds	14 Pounds

Recommended processing time in a weighted-gauge pressure canner:

			PSI At Altitude

Style Of Pack	Size Of Jars	Processing Time	0-100 oft	Above 1000ft
Hot	Pints	70 Minutes	10 Pounds	15 Pounds
Hot	Quarts	90 Minutes	10 Pounds	15 Pounds

Asparagus

Yield: 9 pints
Ingredients:

15-16 pounds needed per canner load.

Directions:

1. Wash the asparagus and trim tough parts.
2. For the hot pack, put the asparagus in boiling water for 2–3 minutes.
3. Fill jars with hot asparagus leaving 1-inch headspace.
4. Pour boiling water, leaving 1-inch headspace.
5. Remove air bubbles.
6. Clean the rims of the jars.
7. Adjust the lids onto the jars and then process.

Recommended Processing Time In A Dial-Gauge Pressure Canner:

Style Of Pack	Size Of Jars	Processing Time	PSI At Altitude			
			0-2000ft	2001-4000ft	4001-6000ft	6001-8000ft
			In Pounds	In Pounds	In Pounds	In Pounds
Hot	Pints	30 Minutes	11 Pounds	12 Pounds	13 Pounds	14 Pounds
Raw	Quarts	40 Minutes	11 Pounds	12 Pounds	13 Pounds	14 Pounds

Recommended Processing Time In A Weighted-Gauge Pressure Canner:

Style Of Pack	Size Of Jars	Processing Time	PSI At Altitude	
			0-1000ft	Above 1000ft
Hot	Pints	30 Minutes	10 Pounds	15 Pounds
Raw	Quarts	8 Minutes	10 pounds	15 pounds

Beans / Peas (All Varieties)

Yield: 9 pints

Ingredients:

3-1/4 pounds of beans
or 5 pounds per canner load of 7 quarts

Directions:

1. Remove any discolored parts from beans or peas.
2. Add the dry beans or peas to a large pot.
3. Pour in water so it submerges.
4. Let it soak for 12 to 18 hours.
5. Now drain the peas or beans.
6. Now, to hydrate the vegetables cover them with boiling water in a large kettle and boil for 2 minutes.
7. Turn off the heat and let it soak for 1 hour and drain.
8. Fill your jars with these beans or peas and pour the cooking water on top, leaving about 1-inch headspace. Remove air bubbles, leaving ¼-inch of headspace.
9. Clean the rims of the jars.
10. Adjust the lids onto the jars and then process.

Recommended processing time in a dial-gauge pressure canner:

			PSI At Altitude			
Style Of Pack	Size Of Jars	Processing Time	0-2000ft	2001-4000ft	4001-6000ft	6000-8000ft
Hot	Pints	70 Minutes	11 Pounds	12 Pounds	13 Pounds	14 Pounds
	Quarts	90 Minutes	11 Pounds	12 Pounds	13 Pounds	14 Pounds

Recommended processing time in a weighted-gauge pressure canner:

			PSI At Altitude	
Style Of Pack	Size Of Jars	Process Time	0-100 0ft	Above 1000ft
Hot	Pints	75 Minutes	10 Pounds	15 Pounds
Hot	Quarts	90 Minutes	10 Pounds	15 Pounds

Corn (Creamy Version)

Yield: 9 pints

Ingredients:

20 pounds ears (in husk), immature kernels

Directions:

1. Husk the corn and remove the silk.
2. Wash the corn ears and blanch the ears in boiling water for 4 minutes.
3. Cut the corn from the cob and remove the kernels.
4. Add water (two cups of water per 1 quart of corn) to a saucepan and bring to the boil.
5. Add ½ teaspoon of salt if liked to each jar.
6. Fill the pint jars with corn mixture, leaving 1-inch of headspace.
7. Remove any air bubbles inside the jar.
8. Clean the rims of the jars.
9. Adjust the lids onto the jars and then process.

Recommended processing time in a dial-gauge pressure canner:

Style Of Pack	Size Of Jars	Processing Time	PSI At Altitude			
			0-2000ft	2001-4000ft	4001-6000ft	6000-8000ft
Hot	Pints	85 Minutes	11pounds	12 Pounds	13 Pounds	14 Pounds

Recommended processing time in a weighted-gauge pressure canner:

Style Of Pack	Size Of Jars	Processing Time	PSI At Altitude	
			0-1000ft	Above 1000ft
Hot	Pints	85 Minutes	10 Pounds	15 Pounds

Category: Tomatoes and Tomato Puree

Tomato Juice

Yield: 9 pints

Ingredients:

14 pounds for 9 pints
1 tablespoon of lemon juice (per pint jar)

Directions:

1. Wash the tomatoes and remove the stems and trim any rotten parts.
2. Remove any discolored parts as well.
3. Quickly cut the tomatoes into quarters and add about a pound to a large saucepan.
4. Keep mashing the tomatoes while it's heating.
5. Continue this step for the remaining pounds.
6. Simmer all the tomatoes for 5 minutes.
7. Press the heated tomatoes through a sieve and collect the juice.
8. Remove the skin and any pulp.
9. Add 1 tablespoon of lemon juice to each pint and pour the tomato juice.
10. Mix and remove any air bubbles, leaving ½-inch headspace.
11. Clean the rims of the jars.
12. Adjust the lids onto the jars and then process.

Note: The pressure canner method results in higher quality.

Recommended processing time in a boiling-water canner:

		Processing Time At Altitude			
Style Of Pack	Size Of Jars	0-1000ft	1001-3000ft	3001-6000ft	Above 6000ft
Hot	Pints	35 Minutes	40 Minutes	45 Minutes	50 Minutes

Recommended processing time in a dial-gauge pressure canner:

			PSI At Altitude			
Style Of Pack	Size Of Jars	Processing Time	0-2000ft	2001-4000ft	4001-6000ft	6000-8000ft

Hot	Pints	20 Minutes	6 Pounds	7 Pounds	8 Pounds	9 Pounds
	Quarts	15 Minutes	11 Pounds	12 Pounds	13 Pounds	14 Pounds

Recommended process time in a weighted-gauge pressure canner:

Style Of Pack	Size Of Jars	Processing Time	PSI At Altitude	
			0-1000ft	Above 1000ft
Hot	Pints	20 Minutes	5 Pounds	10 Pounds

Tomatoes Packed In Water

Yield: 9 pints

Ingredients:

13 pounds tomatoes

Directions:

For raw tomatoes:
1. Wash the tomatoes and dip all the tomatoes in boiling water for 1 minute.
2. Take out all the tomatoes and place them in cold water.
3. Remove the skin and remove the core parts from all the tomatoes.
4. Cut the tomatoes in half or you can leave them as it is.
5. Add 1 tablespoon of lemon juice to each pint and add the tomatoes.
Hot pack:
6. Now for the hot pack product, take a large kettle and add enough water so all the tomatoes are covered.
7. Boil for 5 minutes.
8. Now fill the jars with raw tomatoes or hot tomatoes.
9. Fill the jar with liquid accordingly, for raw boiling water, add liquid from the kettle for hot.
10. Leave about ½-inch headspace.
Note: acidification is needed for pressure canning as well. So, you need to follow the entire step in all methods.
11. Clean the rims of the jars.
12. Adjust the lids onto the jars and then process.

Recommended processing time in a boiling-water canner:

		Processing Time At Altitude			
Style Of Pack	Size Of Jars	0-1000ft	1001-3000ft	3001-6000ft	Above 6000ft
Hot	Pints	40 Minutes	45 Minutes	50 Minutes	55 Minutes

Recommended processing time in a dial-gauge pressure canner:

			PSI At Altitude

Style Of Pack	Size Of Jars	Processing Time	0-2000ft	2001-4000ft	4001-6000ft	6000-8000ft
Hot	Pints	15 Minutes	6 Pounds	7 Pounds	8 Pounds	9 Pounds
	Quarts	10 Minutes	11 Pounds	12 Pounds	13 Pounds	14 Pounds

Recommended processing time in a weighted-gauge pressure canner:

Style Of Pack	Size Of Jars	Processing Time	PSI At Altitude	
			0-1000ft	Above 1000ft
Hot And Raw	Pints	15 Minutes	5 Pounds	10 Pounds

Tomatoes with Okra

Yield: 9 pints

Ingredients:

7 pounds of tomatoes
2-1/2 pounds of okra
(Per canner load of 9 pints)
Use a 3:1 ratio

Directions:

1. Wash both the vegetables.
2. Wash the tomatoes and dip all the tomatoes in boiling water for 1 minute.
3. Take out all the tomatoes and place them in cold water.
4. Remove the skin and remove the core parts from all the tomatoes.
5. Cut the tomatoes in half or you can leave them as it is.
6. Next, trim the stem from the okra and leave it whole or cut it in half.
7. Add tomatoes to a large saucepan and bring it to boil, then add okra.
8. Boil okra for 5 minutes.
9. Add the vegetables to the hot jars leaving 1-inch headspace.
10. Remove any air bubbles and clean the rims.
11. Adjust the lids onto the jars and then process.

Recommended processing time in a dial-gauge pressure canner:

			PSI At Altitude			
Style Of Pack	Size Of Jars	Processing Time	0-2000ft	2001-4000ft	4001-6000ft	6000-8000ft
Hot	Pints	30 Minutes	11Pounds	12 Pounds	13 Pounds	14 Pounds
	Quarts	35 Minutes	11 Pounds	12 Pounds	13 Pounds	14 Pounds

Recommended processing time in a weighted-gauge pressure canner:

			PSI At Altitude	
Style Of Pack	Size Of Jars	Processing Time	0-100oft	Above 1000ft

Hot	Pints	30 Minutes	10Po unds	15 Pounds
quarts	Pints	30 Minutes	10 Pounds	15 Pounds

Category: Pickles and Sauerkraut

Low Sodium Sweet Pickles

Yield: 5 pints

Ingredients:

4 pounds of pickling cucumbers

Ingredients for brine solution:

1-quart white vinegar, distilled (5%)
2 teaspoons of pickling salt
2 teaspoons of mustard seed
1/2 cup granulated sugar

Ingredients for canning syrup:

1-2/3 cups white vinegar, distilled (5%)
3 cups sugar
2 teaspoons of whole allspice
1 tablespoon of celery seed

Directions:

1. Wash the cucumber and cut off the bottom ends and discard.
2. Cut the cucumber into ¼-inch slices.
3. Take a saucepan and add all the canning syrup ingredients to it.
4. Keeps it hot, not boiling.
5. Next, in a kettle, mix all the brining solution ingredients
6. Put the cucumber slices on it, cover, and simmer for 7 minutes.
7. Drain and add to hot jars.
8. Next, pour the canning syrup into sterilized jars.
9. Leave about ½-inch headspace.

10. Remove all the air bubbles.
11. Clean the rims of the jars.
12. Adjust the lids onto the jars and then process.

Recommended processing time in a boiling-water canner:

		Processing Time At Altitude		
Style Of Pack	Size Of Jars	0-1000ft	1001-6000ft	Above 6000ft
Hot	Pints	10 Minutes	15 Minutes	20 Minutes

Low Sodium Dill Pickles

Yield: 8 pints

Ingredients:

4 pounds of pickling cucumbers
6 cups sugar
1 tablespoon of pickling salt
6 cups vinegar, 5%
1-1/2 teaspoons of celery seed
1 tablespoon of mustard seed
2 large onions, thinly sliced
8-9 heads of fresh dill

Directions:

1. Wash the cucumber and cut off the bottom ends and discard.
2. Cut the cucumber into ¼-inch slices.
3. Take a large kettle or saucepan and add sugar, salt, celery seeds, mustard seed, and vinegar and bring it to boil.
4. Add 2 slices of onion and half dill heads to the bottom of each hot jar.
5. Fill the hot, sterilized jars with cucumber slices and leave about ½-inch headspace.
6. Add just a single slice of onion and half of the dill head on top.
7. Add the hot boiling liquid over it leaving ¼-inch headspace.
8. Remove any air bubbles and clean the rims.
9. Adjust the lids onto the jars and then process.

Recommended processing time in a boiling-water canner:

		Processing Time At Altitude		
Style Of Pack	Size Of Jars	0-1000ft	1001-6000ft	Above 6000ft
raw	Pints	15 Minutes	20 Minutes	25 Minutes

Pickled Yellow Peppers

Yield: 4-pint jars

Ingredients:

3 pounds of banana peppers
4-5 teaspoons of celery seed
8 teaspoons of mustard seed
5 cups cider vinegar, (5%)
1-1/4 cups of water
3 tablespoons of canning salt

Directions:

It's recommended to use gloves when completing these procedures.
1. Wash the banana pepper and remove the stem.
2. Cut the pepper into rings about ¼-inch thick.
3. Take a pint jar and add half a tablespoon of celery seed and about 1 tablespoon of mustard seeds.
4. Do the same for all 4 jars.
5. Fill the jars with pepper rings leaving ½-inch headspace.
6. Take a saucepan and add water, salt, and vinegar.
7. Let it boil.
8. Cover the pepper with this boiling water, leaving ¼-inch headspace.
9. Remove any air bubbles and clean the rims.
10. Adjust the lids onto the jars and then process.

Recommended processing time in a boiling-water canner:

		Processing Time At Altitude		
Style Of Pack	Size Of Jars	0-1000ft	1001-6000ft	Above 6000ft
Hot	Pints	10 Minutes	15 Minutes	20Minutes

Pickled Bell Peppers

Yield: 9 pints

Ingredients:

7 pounds of firm bell peppers
3/5 cups of granulated sugar
3 cups white vinegar, (5%)
3 cups water
9-10 cloves of garlic
Pickling salt, as needed

Directions:

1. Wash the pepper and cut it into four parts.
2. Remove seeds and the center.
3. Remove any blemishes.
4. Now cut the parts into strips.
5. Take a pan and add sugar, water, and vinegar.
6. Let it boil for 1 minute.
7. Then add the strips of pepper and boil for 1 minute.
8. Now add about 1 clove of garlic and few pinches of salt to each sterilized jar.
9. Add the pepper strips and hot vinegar, leaving ½-inch of headspace.
10. Remove any air bubbles and clean the rims.
11. Adjust the lids onto the jars and then process.

Recommended processing time in a boiling-water canner:

		Processing Time At Altitude		
Style Of Pack	Size Of Jars	0-1000ft	1001-6000ft	Above 6000ft
Hot	Pints And Half Pints	15 Minutes	20 Minutes	25 Minutes

Pickled Carrots

Yield: 4 pints

Ingredients:

2-3/4 pounds of carrots, washed and peeled
5-1/2 cups white vinegar, 5%
1 cup water
2 cups granulated sugar
2 teaspoons of canning salt
4 tablespoons mustard seed
2 tablespoons celery seed

Directions:

1. Cut the washed and peeled carrots into ½-inch thick rounds.
2. In a saucepan add vinegar, water, and sugar along with salt.
3. Bring it to a boil and simmer for 3–4 minutes.
4. Then add the carrots and boil again.
5. Reduce the heat and simmer for 10 minutes.
6. Meanwhile, add 2 teaspoons of mustard seed and 1 teaspoon of celery seed per pint jar.
7. Then pour the hot carrots and liquid into each jar, leaving 1-inch headspace.
8. Remove any air bubbles and clean the rims.
9. Adjust the lids onto the jars and then process.

Recommended processing time in a boiling-water canner:

Style Of Pack	Size Of Jars	Processing Time At Altitude		
		0-1000ft	1001-6000ft	Above 6000ft
Hot	Pints	15 Minutes	20 Minutes	25 Minutes

Sauerkraut

Yield: 18 pints or 9 quarts

Ingredients:

About 25 pounds of cabbage, fresh and firm
3/4 cup canning salt

Directions:

These recipes are worked in batches, as the cabbage quantity is huge.

1. First, discard the outer leaves of cabbage and rinse the head under water.
2. Drain and then cut the cabbages in quarters, remove the center part of the cabbages.
3. Shred all the cabbages and store in a container for fermentation process, for a 1-gallon container you will need 5 pounds of cabbage, so a 5-gallon stone crock is best suited for this recipe.
4. Now, keep the cabbage 1–2 inches under brine while fermenting it.
5. Place a suitable plate that is smaller than the container, so it covers the cabbage.
6. To keep it on top, add few jars on top and then cover the opening with a heavy towel.
7. Every 3 quarts of water contains about 4.5 tablespoons of salt to make brine.
8. Store it at 50 to 75°F, while it's fermenting.
9. It takes about 4 weeks for sauerkraut to ferment.
10. Once the cabbage is fully fermented, it can be kept in a refrigerator for several months in a sealed, tight pack.

But it can also be canned as followed:

For the hot pack: pour the fermented cabbage and the liquid to a sauce pan and slowly boil it. Stir frequently. Fill the hot jars leaving ½-inch headspace. Clean rims and adjust the lids on top then process as follows.

For the raw pack: first fill the hot jars with fermented cabbage, and cover it with the fermented juices, leaving 1/2-inch headspace. Remove any air bubbles form the jars, clean rims, and adjust the lids on top Then process as follows.

Recommended Processing Time In Boiling Water Canner:

		Processing Time At Altitude			
Style Of Pack	Size Of Jars	0-1000ft	1001-3000ft	3001-6000ft	Above 6000ft
	Pints	10 Minutes	15 Minutes	15 Minutes	20 Minutes
Hot	Quarts	15 Minutes	20 Minutes	20 Minutes	25 Minutes
	Pints	20 Minutes	25 Minutes	30 Minutes	35 Minutes
Raw					

	Quarts	25 Minutes	30 Minutes	35 Minutes	40 Minutes

No Sugar Added Pickled Beets

Yield: 8 Pints

Ingredients:

7 pounds of beets, cut into 2 inches diameter
6 cups white vinegar, 5%
1-1/2 teaspoon pickling salt
2 cups Splenda
3 cups water
3 cinnamon sticks
14 whole cloves

Directions:

1. Trim off the beets and cut the top, cube into 2-inch pieces.
2. Wash the cubes well.
3. Boil water in a large kettle and add beets.
4. Let it cook for 30 minutes.
5. Then drain and set the beets aside for cooling.
6. Mix the vinegar, salt, Splenda, and 3 cups of fresh water in a large saucepan oven.
7. Tie the cinnamon stick and cloves to cheesecloth and add it as well.
8. Bring this mixture to a boil.
9. Remove the cinnamon and clove cheesecloth bag.
10. Add the beets to the hot jar and pour the vinegar liquid over.
11. Make sure no bubbles form inside, leaving enough space on top of about ½ inches.
12. Clean the rims.
13. Adjust the lids onto the jars and then process.

Recommended Processing Time In Boiling Water Canner:

Style Of Pack	Size Of Jars	Processing Time At Altitude			
		0-1000ft	1001-3000ft	3001-6000 ft	Above 6000ft
Hot	Pints Or Half Pints	30 Minutes	35 Minutes	40 Minutes	45 Minutes

Category: Jams, Jellies

Berries Jam

Yield: 3-4 Half Pints

Ingredients:

4 cups crushed strawberries
4 cups of sugar, granulated

Directions:

1. Place a plate in the freezer to let it get cold.
2. Remove the cap of the strawberries and crush it.
3. Add strawberries to a saucepan and add sugar.
4. Boil it until it is thickened.
5. Now test the doneness, for that, take out the cold plate and pour a drop of liquid on it, if the mixture is jelly-like, then it's done.
6. Remove it from heat and skim any foam from the top.
7. Ladle the prepared jam into the sterilized jars, using fennel, and make sure no bubbles form inside, leaving enough space on top about ½-inch.
8. Clean the rims.
9. Adjust the lids onto the jars and then process.

Recommended processing time in a boiling-water canner:

		Processing Time At Altitude		
Style Of Pack	Size Of Jars	0-1000ft	1001-6000ft	Above 6000ft
Hot	Pints Or Half Pints	5 Minutes	10 Minutes	15 Minutes

Blackberries Vanilla Jam

Yield: 4 half-pint jars

Ingredients:

4 cups of fresh blackberries
4 cup white sugar, granulated
1-2 tablespoons lemon juice
1/4 vanilla bean pod, seeds scraped

Directions:

1. Place a plate in the freezer to let it get cold.
2. Wash the blackberries and crush them, then add them to a saucepan and add sugar.
3. Boil it until it is thickened.
4. Now test the doneness, for that, take out the freezer plate and pour a drop of liquid on it.
5. If the mixture is gel textured, then it's done.
6. Remove it from heat and skim any foam on top.
7. Mix in vanilla and lemon juice.
8. Stir well.
9. Ladle the prepared jam into sterilized jars, using fennel, and make sure no bubbles form inside, leaving enough space on top of about ½-inch.
10. Remove any air bubbles and clean the rims.
11. Adjust the lids onto the jars and then process.

Recommended processing time in a boiling-water canner:

		Processing Time At Altitude		
Style Of Pack	Size Of Jars	0-1000ft	1001-6000ft	Above 6000ft
Hot	Pints or half pints	5 Minutes	10 Minutes	15 Minutes

Apple and Pear Jam (With Pectin)

Yield: 7 Half Pints

Ingredients:

2 pounds of pears, peeled, cored, and chopped
1 cup apples, peeled, chopped and seeds removed
6.5 cups sugar
1/4 teaspoon ground cinnamon
1/3 cup lemon juice, bottled
6 ounces of liquid pectin

Directions

1. Crush the apples and pears in a large saucepan.
2. Mix in lemon juice, cinnamon, and sugar.
3. Bring this mixture to a boil.
4. Keep stirring the ingredients.
5. Stir in pectin.
6. Bring it to a rolling boil and let it hard boil for 1 minute.
7. Stir constantly.
8. Then remove the scum formed on the top and remove it from heat.
9. Fill the sterilized jars with it, leaving 1/4-inch headspace.
10. Clean the rims of jars.
11. Remove any air bubbles.
12. Adjust the lids onto the jars and then process.

Recommended processing time in a boiling-water canner:

		Processing Time At Altitude		
Style Of Pack	Size Of Jars	0-1000ft	1001-6000ft	Above 6000ft
Hot	Pints or half pints	5 Minutes	10 Minutes	15 Minutes

Apple jelly without Pectin

Yield: 4-5 Half Pint jars

Ingredients:

4 pounds of apples
4 cups water
3 cups of sugar

Directions:

1. Freeze one plate in a freezer for testing the jelly texture.
2. Use firm apples and wash them well.
3. Then peel the apples and remove the seeds.
4. Then chop the apples.
5. Add the apples and water to a large saucepan.
6. Let it boil and then simmer for 20–25 minutes.
7. Then strain the liquid through a sieve and press the pulp as much as possible, to get out the extract.
8. It would result in 4–6 cups of juice.
9. Now pour the juice back into the saucepan.
10. Now add sugar and let it boil unit a jelly texture is obtained.
11. Now test the doneness, for that, take out a freezer plate and pour a drop of liquid on it.
12. If the mixture is gel-like, then it's done.
13. Ladle the prepared jelly into the sterilized jars, using fennel, and make sure no bubbles form inside, leaving enough space on top of about ½-inch.
14. Adjust the lids onto the jars and then process.

Recommended processing time in a boiling-water canner:

Style Of Pack	Size Of Jars	Processing Time At Altitude		
		0-1000ft	1001-6000ft	Above 6000ft
Hot	Pints or half pints	5 Minutes	10 Minutes	15 Minutes

Grape and Plum Jelly

Yield: 10 half pint jars

Ingredients:

3.5 pounds of ripe plums
3 pounds of grapes, ripe
1 cup water
8.5 cups granulated white sugar
1.75 ounces of powdered pectin

Directions:

1. Wash the plums and grapes.
2. Do not peel the plums.
3. Crush the plums and grapes.
4. Put all of it into a saucepan.
5. Then add water.
6. Bring it to a boil.
7. Then simmer for 10 minutes.
8. Strain this mixture through double-layered cheesecloth.
9. It should give 6–7 cups of juice.
10. Add it to a saucepan and bring it to a boil.
11. Add the pectin to the saucepan and hard boil.
12. Now add the sugar and let it full boil.
13. Then simmer for 1 minute.
14. Stir it constantly.
15. Collect any foam formed on top and fill sterilized jars with it by leaving 1/4-inch headspace.
16. Remove any air bubbles and clean the rims.
17. Adjust the lids onto the jars and then process.

Recommended processing time in boiling-water canners:

		Processing Time At Altitude		
Style Of Pack	Size Of Jars	0-1000ft	1001-6000ft	Above 6000ft
Hot	Pints Or Half Pints	5 Minutes	10 Minutes	15 Minutes

Category: Sweet Spread

Apples and grapes are sweet fruits, so a sweetener containing low calories is added to the recipe. The gelatin is used as thickening agent. So, the jars should not be processed and only refrigerated. It is recommended to consume it within four weeks.

Grape Sweet Spread (Gelatin)

Yield: 3 Half Pints

Ingredients:

4 teaspoons of gelatin powder, unflavored
24 ounces of unsweetened grape juice
4 teaspoons of bottled lemon juice
4 teaspoons of low-calorie sweetener

Directions:

1. Take a large saucepan and add softened gelatin along with lemon juice and grapes.
2. Bring this mixture to a rolling boil until the gelatin is dissolved.
3. Boil it for a minute and remove it from the heat.
4. Stir in the sweetener.
5. Now fill the hot jars with the mixture, leaving ¼-inch of headspace.
6. Clean the rims.
7. Adjust the lids onto the jars.
8. Do not process or freeze it.
9. Once it has cooled down, store in the refrigerator.
It can be used for 4 weeks.

Refrigerated Apple Spread (With Gelatin)

Yield: 4 Half Pints

Ingredients:

4 teaspoons of unflavored gelatin powder
4 cups of unsweetened apple juice
4 teaspoons of bottled lemon juice
4 teaspoons of sweetener
2 sticks of cinnamon

Directions:

1. Take a large saucepan and add softened gelatin along with cinnamon sticks, lemon juice and apple juice.
2. Bring this mixture to a rolling boil until the gelatin has dissolved.
3. Boil it for a minute and remove it from the heat.
4. Stir in the sweetener.
5. Now fill the hot jars with the mixture leaving ¼-inch of headspace.
6. Clean the rims.
7. Adjust the lids onto the jars.
8. Do not process or freeze it.
9. Once it has cooled down, store in the refrigerator.

It can be used for 4 weeks.

Pineapple and Peach Spread

Yield: 5 Half Pint Jars

Ingredients:

4 cups peach pulp
2 cups pineapple
¼ cup bottled lemon juice
2 cups sugar

Directions:

1. Crush the peaches and add them to a saucepan.
2. Now cook the fruit on low, until it releases juices.
3. Place this cooked peach into a jelly bag and let it pass juice for 15 minutes.
4. Now mix the collected 4 cups of pulp from the jelly bag with pineapple and lemon in a saucepan.
5. Keep the collected juice for some other purposes like making jelly.
6. Add sugar and mix.
7. Heat it for 15 minutes.
8. Fill hot jars loosely with raw meat pieces, leaving 1/4-inch headspace. Do not add liquid.
9. Clean the rims and clean the jars,
10. Adjust the lids onto the jars and then process.

Notes: This recipe can also be made without sugar.

Recommended Processing Time In Boiling Water Canner:

		Processing Time At Altitude			
Style Of Pack	Size Of Jars	0-1000ft	1001-3000ft	3001-6000 Ft	Above 6000ft
Hot	Half Pints	15 Minutes	20 Minutes	20 Minutes	25 Minutes
	Pints	20 Minutes	25 Minutes	30 Minutes	35 Minutes

Category: Meat, Poultry, and Fish

Chicken

Yield: 6-8 half pints jars

Ingredients:

2 pounds of chicken

Directions:

Use only fresh chicken.
Use a large chicken.
1. Remove any excess fat from the chicken.
2. Fill the hot jars with pieces of chicken and broth.
3. Leave ¼-inch head space.

Raw pack:

1. Add just a teaspoon salt per quart of the jar, (optional).
2. Now fill the hot jars with meat and leave ¼-inch of headspace.
3. Do not add the liquid.

For both packs:
1. Fill hot jars loosely with raw meat pieces, leaving 1/4-inch headspace. Do not add liquid.
2. Clean the rims and clean the jars,
3. Adjust the lids onto the jars and then process.

Recommended processing time in a dial-gauge pressure canner:

Style Of Pack	Size Of Jars	Process Time	PSI At Altitude			
			0-2000ft	2001-4000ft	4001-6000ft	6000-8000ft
Hot and raw	Pints	75 Minutes	11pounds	12 Pounds	13 Pounds	14 Pounds
	Quarts	90 Minutes	11 Pounds	12 Pounds	13 Pounds	14 Pounds

Recommended processing time in a weighted-gauge pressure canner:

Style Of Pack	Size Of Jars	Processing Time	PSI At Altitude	
			0-1000ft	Above 1000ft
Hot And Raw	Pints	75Minutes	10 Pounds	15 Pounds
	Quarts	90 Minutes	10 Pounds	15 Pounds

Meat

Ingredients:

Beef meat, as needed

Directions:

1. Choose high-quality meat and cut away all the fat.
2. Remove the large bones and then hot pack the meat for best quality.
3. For that, cook the meat by roasting or stewing it.
4. Add some salt, just a teaspoon, per quart to the jar.
5. Fill hot jars with meat pieces and add meat drippings or tomato juice.
6. Remove air bubbles and leave almost 1-inch headspace in jars.
7. Clean the rims.
8. Tightly pack the jars and process.

For raw pack: Add the raw meat pieces to the jars leaving a 1-inch headspace.

Recommended processing time in a dial-gauge pressure canner:

Style Of Pack	Size Of Jars	Processing Time	PSI At Altitude			
			0-2000ft	2001-4000ft	4001-6000ft	6000-8000ft
Hot And Raw Both	Pints	75 Minutes	11pounds	12 Pounds	13 Pounds	14 Pounds
	Quarts	90 Minutes	11pounds	12 Pounds	13 Pounds	14 Pounds

Recommended processing time in a weighted-gauge pressure canner:

Style Of Pack	Size Of Jars	Process Time	PSI At Altitude	
			0-1000ft	Above 1000ft
Raw and hot	Pints	75 Minutes	10 Pounds	15 Pounds
	quarts	90 Minutes	10 Pounds	15 Pounds

Fish in Pint Jars

Ingredients:

Trout Fish wild-caught, as needed
Salt, as needed

Directions:

1. Clean the fish and place it on ice until needed to can.
2. Rinse the fresh fish and add vinegar during rinsing to remove the bad odor.
3. Remove the tail, scales, and heat.
4. Cut the fish lengthwise and then into 3 1/2-inch pieces.
5. Add it to hot jars leaving 1-inch headspace.
6. Add 1 teaspoon salt, per pint if liked.
7. No need to add liquid.
8. Clean the jar and rims
9. Seal it tight and process.

Recommended processing time in a dial-gauge pressure canner:

Style Of Pack	Size Of Jars	Process ing Time	PSI At Altitude			
			0-2000ft	2001-4 000ft	4001-6 000ft	6000-8000ft
Raw	Pints	100 Minutes	11 Pounds	12 Pounds	13 Pounds	14 Pounds

Recommended processing time in a weighted-gauge pressure canner:

Style Of Pack	Size Of Jars	Processi ng Time	PSI At Altitude	
			0-1000 ft	Above 1000ft
raw	Pints	100 Minutes	10 Pounds	15 Pounds

Category: Soups and Stews

Chile Con Carne
Yield: 9 pints

Ingredients:

3 cups of red kidney beans
5.5 cups water
2 tablespoons of salt (divided)
3 pounds of ground beef
1.5 cups of onions, chopped
1 cup peppers, chopped
1 teaspoon of grounded black pepper
4 tablespoons of chili powder
2 quarts of tomatoes, crushed

Directions:

1. Wash the red beans and add them to a saucepan.
2. Pour in the water 3 inches above the beans.
3. Soak it overnight.
4. The next day, discard the water.
5. Now, add beans to a large pot and pour in water and half of the salt.
6. Let it boil and simmer for 25–30 minutes.
7. Drain water and set it aside.
8. Take a skillet and brown the beef and onion.
9. Then add peppers.
10. Now add salt, tomatoes, pepper, chili powder, and beans.
11. Cook for 5 minutes.
12. It should not be cooked to the thickness.
13. Now pour it into hot jars, leaving 1-inch headspace.
14. Remove air bubbles.
15. Clean rims.
16. Adjust the lids onto the jars and then process.

Recommended processing time in a dial-gauge pressure canner:

Style Of Pack	Size Of Jars	Process Time	PSI At Altitude			
			0-2000ft	2001-4000ft	4001-6000ft	6000-8000ft
Hot	Pints	75 Minutes	11pounds	12 Pounds	13 Pounds	14 Pounds

Recommended processing time in a weighted-gauge pressure canner:

			PSI At Altitude	
Style Of Pack	Size Of Jars	Processing Time	0-1000ft	Above 1000ft
Hot	Pints	75 Minutes	10 Pounds	15 Pounds

Meat Stock

Yield: 4-5 half pints jars

Ingredients:

10 pounds trimmed beef bones
12 cups of water

Directions:

1. Rinse the bones and add them to a large Dutch oven, pour in the water so it covers, and simmer for 5 hours.
2. Remove the bones and cool the broth.
3. Pass the broth from the sieve and discard any fat or scum collected at the top.
4. Remove any meat tidbits.
5. Reheat the broth for a few minutes; it will simmer down in quantity.
6. Pour it into jars leaving 1-inch headspace.
7. Wipe the jar rims.
8. Adjust the lids onto the jars and then process.

Recommended processing time in a dial-gauge pressure canner:

			PSI At Altitude			600 0-8000 ft
Style Of Pack	Size Of Jars	Processing Time	0-2000 ft	2001-4000ft	4001-6000ft	
Hot	Pints	20 Minutes	11 Pounds	12 Pounds	13 Pounds	14 Pounds
	Quarts	25 Minutes	11 Pounds	12 Pounds	13 Pounds	14 Pounds

Recommended processing time in a weighted-gauge pressure canner:

			PSI At Altitude	
Style Of Pack	Size Of Jars	Process Time	0-1000ft	Above 1000ft
Hot	Pints	2 Minutes	10 Pounds	15 Pounds

5

Conversion Chart

Spoons	
16 tablespoons	1 cup
1 tablespoon	1/16 cup
12 tablespoons	3/4 cup
2 tablespoons	1/8 cup
10 tablespoons	2/3 cup
4 tablespoons	1/4 cup
5 tablespoons	1/3 cup
8 tablespoons	1/2 cup

Weight		
Grams	Ounces	Cups
15	0.5	
25	0.9	
50	1.8	
75	2.6	0.33
100	3.5	
150	5.3	0.67
175	6.2	
200	7.1	
225	7.9	1
250	8.8	

275	9.7	
300	10.6	1.33
350	12.3	
375	13.2	1.67
400	14.1	1.75
425	15	
450	15.9	2
500	17.6	
700	24.7	
750	26.5	3
1000	35.3	
1250	44.1	5.5
1500	52.9	
2000	70.5	9

Volume: Liquid Conversion

Metric	Imperial	USA
250ml	8 fl oz	1 cup
150ml	5 fl oz	2/3 cup
120ml	4 fl oz	1/2 cup
75ml	2 1/2 fl oz	1/3 cup
60ml	2 fl oz	1/4 cup
15ml	1/2 fl oz	1 tablespoon

180ml	6 fl oz	3/4 cup

Temperatures		
°C	°F	
110	230	
120	250	
130	265	
140	285	
150	300	
160	320	
170	340	
180	355	
190	375	
200	390	
210	410	
220	430	
230	445	
240	464	
250	482	

Liquids			
Gallon	Quarts	Pints	Cups
1	4	8	16
1/2	2	4	8
1/4	1	2	4
1/8	1/2	1	2

Conclusion

Canning food is a healthy way to keep food fresh and nutritious. Choosing to go back and adopt simple ways of living is what this book is about. Preserving food is a great technique that Amish communities love to do, and we are privileged to avail their knowledge and expertise to create USDA guidelines-approved recipes that can be stored for years-long use.

Now you can learn different canning methods, as this book provides all the necessary information to make the transaction smooth. You get not only the basics of Amish canning but also learn the techniques and different canning methods with some wholesome recipes to try. Gain peace of mind by saving money through food preservation in the form of canning.

We hope this book serves you all in every aspect from learning about Amish canning, to the basics of canning, and implementing some home canning techniques to preserve fruits, pickles, jams, jellies, and meat items.

Thank You

I just wanted to say how much I appreciate you.

I couldn't continue to produce useful publications like this one without your support and interest in them.

THANK YOU AGAIN for reading this book. Hope you liked it as much as I had fun writing it.

I need you to do me a little favor before you leave.

Would you kindly think about publishing a book review for this one on the platform?

My writing will be supported by reviews.

Your comments are very valuable to me and will enable me to produce more. Upcoming works of informational literature.

I'm interested in hearing from you.

Guinevere.

Made in the USA
Monee, IL
06 December 2024

72640996R00050